# THE FIGHTING WEAPONS
# OF KOREAN MARTIAL ARTS

By In Hyuk Suh and Jane Hallander

## DISCLAIMER

Although both Unique Publications and the author(s) of this martial arts book have taken great care to ensure the authenticity of the information and techniques contained herein, we are not responsible, in whole or in part, for any injury which may occur to the reader or readers by reading and/or following the instructions in this publication. We also do not guarantee that the techniques and illustrations described in this book will be safe and effective in a self-defense or training situation. It is understood that there exists a potential for injury when using or demonstrating the techniques herein described. It is essential that before following any of the activities, physical or otherwise, herein described, the reader or readers first should consult his or her physician for advice on whether practicing or using the techniques described in this publication could cause injury, physical or otherwise. Since the physical activities described herein could be too sophisticated in nature for the reader or readers, it is essential a physician be consulted. Also, federal, state or local laws may prohibit the use or possession of weapons described herein. A thorough examination must be made of the federal, state and local laws before the reader or readers attempts to use these weapons in a self-defense situation or otherwise. Neither Unique Publications nor the author(s) of this martial arts book guarantees the legality or the appropriateness of the techniques or weapons herein contained.

## UNIQUE PUBLICATIONS

4201 Vanowen Place
Burbank, CA 91505

ISBN: 0-86568-076-0
Library of Congress Catalog No. 85-52273

**Designer:** Danilo J. Silverio
**Editors:** Sandra Segal and Dave Cater

TABLE OF CONTENTS

FOREWORD

The study of Korean martial arts goes much further than bare-hand or foot self-defense. Throughout history, weapons have played a major role in all martial arts. Weapons training gave the ancient fighter a sharper cutting edge and longer reach, and improved his strength, balance, coordination and focus.

Many weapons serve as weight-training devices. Constant practice with a staff will surely strengthen a martial artist's wrists, forearms and shoulders, while increasing the flexibility of his back and waist.

Any weapon which adds weight to one hand will teach its bearer a lesson in balance. It is tough enough to remain stable and balanced while moving rapidly through a form when bare-handed. It becomes even more difficult with the additional weight of a sword in one hand. Not only does the hand holding the sword need to compensate for the extra weight, but the free hand must also make adjustments. Many martial arts students suddenly realize how useless their other hand has become when they put a weapon in one hand.

When placed in the position of having to wield two weapons at once, the student must learn coordination between his two hands, something hard to come by in empty-hand practice.

The primary principle of all weapons is to put their striking surface exactly where it's aimed, a point often missed by those practicing fist forms. It is difficult to develop focus without a target. When practicing with a weapon, there is always a target, even though it's imaginary. Focus and intention are the results.

One final reason to study weapons: When interest lags after running through the hand form for the 100th time, it's a nice change of pace to pick up a sword, fan or staff.

# CHAPTER ONE

# Korea's Ancient Warriors

It is known warriors from any culture rely upon weapons knowledge as the backbone of their fighting art. Japan's samurai class were known not for their bare-fisted ability but instead for their superb swordsmanship. The same was true for China and its smaller neighbor, Korea. Battles were won by martial artists equipped with spears and swords, while bare-handed and kicking techniques were reserved for last-ditch defense, when the fighter's weapon was lost or destroyed.

Since many of the ancient weapons techniques were basically extensions of the martial artist's hands, they formed a foundation around which much empty-hand combat evolved. The same is true today. With the basic knowledge of Korean fan or short-stick movements, a person can pick up a rolled magazine and apply many of the same techniques toward self-defense.

Legend has it that in 2330 B.C., Dan Koon Wang Kum, the first ruler of the unified land mass later to be named *Korea*, brought together the many scattered tribes into one kingdom, called *Ko Chosun (Old Korea)*.

History indicates tribes gradually migrated into what is now Korea looking for good climate, fertile farm lands, plentiful fishing areas, and the excellent hunting provided by Korea's low sloping mountains. Since many different tribes inhabited a small peninsula of land, it was necessary for each tribe to maintain well-trained warriors to protect their people.

Dan Koon Wang Kum was a true warrior king who used his martial arts and military knowledge to bring four hostile territories — Nan Nang, Jin Bun, Im Doon, and Hyun Doo — together to form the unified Ko Chosun kingdom. The empire lasted 12 centuries.

Tracing directly to the Ko Chosun kingdom was Korea's oldest foundation martial art, *sado mu sool* (tribal or family martial art). Each warlord, territory, and village in the days of Ko Chosun had its private armies, utilizing sado mu sool techniques.

The first weapon of early sado mu sool was the simple stone. From the stone came stone knives, stone spears, and stone axes. Sado mu sool was characterized by its weapons-throwing techniques, called *too suk sool*, using rocks, stone implements, and even sand. So effective were these techniques they formed one of the primary defensive techniques used against the Japanese in the battles at the Hangji and Chinju mountain fortresses during Hideoshi's invasion of Korea in the late 15th century.

The period following the Ko Chosun kingdom was called the Three Kingdom era (18 B.C.-A.D. 918) and was comprised of three separate governing kingdoms, Paekje, Koguryo, and Silla.

Martial arts grew rapidly during the Three Kingdom period for several reasons. First, Koguryo, Paekje, and Silla were constantly at war with one another, which forced the young men of each kingdom to become well-versed in martial arts. Sado mu sool was the predominant fighting style among the working-class warriors.

The second factor forcing martial arts development during this period was that government positions were filled according to the fighting ability of the individual, not his scholarly capabilities. The king and provincial governors were commander-in-chiefs of the armies and high-ranking warriors who were responsible for defense of the kingdom as well as political and judicial governing.

At that time special village military guards, called *doo rai*, were commonplace. Doo rai groups were sado mu sool practitioners responsible for maintaining order within each village. They still relied primarily upon too suk sool.

Later during the Koryo Kingdom (A.D. 918-1393), these same sado mu sool doo rai units became privately organized armies used in the many power struggles between Koryo warlords.

In 987, the Koryo king, Sung Jong, decreed only the government militia could carry weapons. Sado mu sool private armies became bodyguard units (called *sa byung*), designed to provide personal protection for high-ranking generals and political officials.

One of the first orders of Sung Kye Lee, who overthrew the Koryo Kingdom in 1393, was to disband all private armies. However, many sado mu sool groups secretly carried on their martial art in the rural areas of Korea.

*Bulkyo mu sool* (Buddhist martial art) was the

second prominent Korean foundation martial art. It was first recorded in the Koguryo Kingdom (one of the kingdoms of the Three Kingdom era) about A.D. 347. Soon after, Bulkyo mu sool found its way into Paekje and Silla, the other two powers of the Three Kingdoms.

Bulkyo mu sool was originally developed to promote better health among the sedentary, meditation-oriented Buddhist monks. Since the monks spent a major portion of their waking hours meditating in sitting positions on cold wooden floors, digestive and circulatory problems easily developed. To overcome those maladies, Buddhist monks instigated special lower abdomen breathing patterns and concentrated upon internal or *ki* development to balance their internal organs. Added to internal development were physical exercises utilizing the staff and cane, common implements of Buddhist monks in Korea.

In 1592, during the Lee dynasty (1392-1910), a strange event occurred. Japan invaded Korea for the first time; an opportune invasion since Korea depended solely upon its friendship and treaty with Tang dynasty China for military protection. While the Chinese did send troops to defend Korea from the invading Japanese, the long overland trip kept them from reaching the battlefields in time.

However, an army of over 9,000 Buddhist monks massed together under one leader, a monk named Won-Hyo Sosan, in time to play a major role in repulsing the Japanese. These fighting monks comprised a major portion of an army called *ui bying (righteous army)*, a militia force formed partly through a defensive need and partly from a strong sense of loyalty and patriotism.

Since Korea's own army was poorly equipped to fight the well-organized Japanese invaders, it became the task of Won-Hyo Sosan and his lieutenant, another fighting monk named Sa-Myong-Dong, to organize and train Buddhist monks in the martial arts necessary to defend their nation. They were successful in repulsing the Japanese, and from that time, Buddhist monks were collectively known as *defenders of the nation*, playing prominent roles in the defense and martial arts of Korea. Only in Korea were Orthodox Buddhist monks allowed *by their religion* to actively learn and practice a fighting art.

Many staff and cane techniques seen in modern kuk sool won training forms draw their roots from the teaching of Bulkyo mu sool monks and from the needs of Korea's so-called *beggar monks*.

When a monk first became ordained in Buddhism, he was given the task of proving his lack of attachment to material things by begging for alms from village to village. The roads between villages were often prime areas for the activities of robbers and thugs who would attack *anyone*, including the poor begging monks. For their protection, along with staff and cane techniques, special joint-locking and pressure-point fighting tactics were used for purposes of *submission*, not killing (Buddhism prohibits the wanton taking of lives).

These submission techniques have become one of the foundations of modern Korean martial arts, such as kuk sool won. They are commonly employed by Korean police units, often in conjunction with the use of short sticks, as safe methods of disarming and apprehending dangerous felons.

The third important foundation martial art was called *koong joong mu sool* (royal palace martial arts), which had its beginnings during the Three Kingdom era.

The *sun bi* ("intelligent brave" warriors) of the Koguryo Kingdom represented koong joong mu sool in the military hierarchy. They carried five short knives (*dan gum*) hidden in the waistband of their garments with which they were prepared at any moment to defend their royal masters.

To join the ranks of the sun bi warriors, a fighter was required to study bow and arrow, long sword, horsemanship, knife throwing, hand-to-hand combat, combat under water, hunting, fishing, politics, music, and classical literature. Only after passing tests in these disciplines were they awarded the rank of *sun bi*.

The Paekje Kingdom also had its sun bi equivalents. In 320, Paekje king Bi-ryu had a special martial arts center built for the exclusive use of his personal royal court warriors. Training within this center consisted of horsemanship, *bong* (staff) fighting, swordsmanship, empty-hand fighting, Buddhism, and classical literature.

The Paekje Kingdom maintained a strong trading policy with ancient Japan and is reputed to have furnished Japan with many cultural and military advances, such as swordsmanship (the forerunner of Japan's samurai system) and staff techniques.

Meanwhile, on the southeast corner of the Korean peninsula, the Silla Kingdom bred a new form of koong joong mu sool fighter. These were highly trained scholars who were as proficient at fighting as they were at penmanship. Known as *wha rang* (flower of youth), they were young men who had been chosen to become Silla's future military leaders.

Wha rangs believed a healthy body brings about a healthy spirit, and vice-versa. Toward that end, wha rang groups trained throughout the year in Korea's wild rugged mountains or along its desolate shores.

Wha rang fighters had a five-point code of conduct around which they structured their lives. The five points were:

**1)** Be loyal to king and country.

**2)** Be obedient to your parents.

**3)** Be honorable to your friends.

**4)** Kill justly.

**5)** *Never* retreat in battle.

The last point, *never retreat in battle*, won everlasting fame in Korean history for the wha rang warriors, who were known as the Silla Kingdom's most fearless fighters.

In 688, the Silla Kingdom, with help from China, overthrew both the Paekje and Koguryo Kingdoms and unified them into one Korea under Silla rule. At that time, in retribution for its help to the Silla king, China annexed a large portion of the former Koguryo Kingdom. This section of land later became known as Manchuria. Since that piece of land, as large as the present-day Korean peninsula, had represented Korean culture and martial arts for so long and has now been a part of China for hundreds of years, it is difficult to say whether the martial arts of Korea and that portion of China are distinct representatives of their individual countries or perhaps combinations of both cultures, thrown together and blended throughout the years.

Approximately 500 years ago, midway through the Lee dynasty, the Korean Royal Court officially adopted 24 of Korea's many different weapons as weapons of koong joong mu sool. Because of the strong political ties with China at the time, 18 of those 24 Royal Court weapons were the same weapons commonly seen in traditional Chinese martial arts.

In 1790, a Lee dynasty king named Jung Jo ordered written a book called *Mooye Dohbo Tongji.* Its purpose was to describe Korean martial arts techniques. This famous document illustrates the use of various types of spear techniques, both from horseback and on the ground, military swords, staffs, and even weaponless combat, including pressure-point strikes.

Koong joong mu sool dominated Korean martial arts until 1910, when Japanese armies occupied Korea and began their reign of cultural genocide.

Koreans were forbidden to speak their native language in public places; only Japanese could be spoken. Many of the trees covering Korea's hills were cut down and the lumber shipped to Japan, creating a desolate appearance.

Martial arts were outlawed, and all weapons, even antiques, were sent out of the country or melted down for use in Japanese factories.

However, martial arts did survive. Important martial artists, such as Royal Court Army Master Instructor Myung Duk Suh, my grandfather, practiced their martial expertise in secret and passed it on to dedicated disciples.

After World War II, martial arts in Korea were just beginning to restructure when the Korean conflict struck, and everything returned to chaos.

After eight long years of warfare and destruction, the Korean conflict ended, and South Korea emerged as a separate nation with a fragile economy and much building to be done. Martial arts had been reduced to the activities of common street thugs and had gained the reputation of *gangster training*.

Gradually, through the efforts of a few individuals whose traditional training had survived both the Japanese and Korean conflicts, the traditional martial arts of Korea, combining mental and physical training to produce a better individual, were returned to the Korean public.

In the late 1950s the traditional fighting art techniques of Korea were organized into a single martial art, called *kuk sool won (Korean national martial art association)*. Founded by myself, kuk sool won became one of the first traditional martial arts schools to be opened to the Korean public.

Kuk sool won was organized as a *martial art* organization in 1961. Kuk sool won is currently the largest Korean martial arts organization in the world (tae kwon do is recognized in Korea by both the Korean government and the World Tae Kwon Do federation as a martial *sport*), with over 200 schools in South Korea and well over 100 throughout the United States and the rest of the world. All kuk sool won schools are standardized, ensuring traditional techniques are kept pure and unchanged.

Kuk sool won is also the only Korean martial system to teach all 24 of Korea's traditional *royal court* weapons as an important segment of its overall program. Weapons techniques from sado mu sool, Buldo mu sool, and koong joong mu sool are taught to both maintain the Korean cultural heritage and give the kuk sool won student an idea of the practical use of ancient martial arts weapons.

# CHAPTER TWO

# Sado Mu Sool's Sword

Korea actually has a long martial history filled with the weapons that have given Japan and China their traditional martial flavor. The most prominent weapon is the sword.

In the early period of sado mu sool, weapons constructed of stone played important roles. While throwing stones were one of the first methods of hunting, the hunters still needed to cut apart the carcasses of the animals they killed, hence the development of a stone knife and stone ax. Soon sado mu sool warriors discovered the advantages of stabbing and slicing weapons, sparking the evolution of the sword.

Korea's first metal swords were initially described in early writings of the Paekje Kingdom (A.D. 200). Of the three kingdoms, Paekje was the power to have the most contact with Japan, and it was then that steel and bronze swords found their way from

Korea into Japan to feed that nation's thirst for sharp metal fighting implements.

The sword (*gum* in Korean) was so special to Korean martial arts that during the Three Kingdom period, great swordsmen were singled out with honor and respect. At the same time, a poor swordsman was considered so despicable he was pitied.

Unlike Japan and China, where sword shapes followed a certain pattern and design, based primarily on their use, Korean blades evolved as mirror images of the swordsman who owned the weapon. Many martial artists made their swords, and they created all sorts of sizes and shapes. Swords became so varied it was impossible to make one using a set pattern. Korean swords were very personal and individual weapons, crafted to fit the strength and body

characteristics of their owner.

Lengths ranged from short knifelike blades to the more common longer weapons. The shape most often seen was a double-edged straight sword, similar to the Chinese straight sword, but bearing a thicker, heavier blade.

Three types of swords originated within the sado mu sool structure of Korea's martial history. These swords are named *not for their shape*, but for the fighting techniques they employ. *Jun gum* refers to straight linear-motion techniques. *Yuk gum* means inverted (with the cutting edge of the blade positioned up, rather than down) techniques. *Jang san gum* techniques employ both straight and circular techniques, performed with long double swords.

The first sword principle taught in kuk sool won is jun gum. Jun gum lays the basis and foundation for all sword training. The term *straight sword* does not refer to the shape of the blade. Instead, it defines the action and movements made by the sword practitioner.

Jun gum techniques are straight-line slicing, chopping and thrusting actions. Rather than just another weapon to learn, the sword is always considered the result of earlier basic training principles. Thus, the swordplay of ancient Korea's martial artists reflected the background and knowledge of their many years in martial arts.

Korean swordsmanship is based on five tactical theories, called *jwa sae* (position), which form the foundation for control, calmness and effectiveness. Without jwa sae training, a student cannot properly master swordsmanship.

Jwa sae actually defines the martial artist's position with relation to the events around him, both physically and mentally. Jwa sae can be a series of defensive and offensive movements relating to his situation, or it can be the self-training of meditation and *ki* (internal energy) development. Jwa sae can also be each movement within a *hyung*. Jwa sae means each mental and physical position has its definite purpose at the moment of use.

Jwa sae is further broken into five subprinciples, each an important and necessary part of jwa sae. They combine to become the complete concept of jwa sae with a sword in hand.

The five jwa sae subprinciples are:

**1)** Eyes — The martial artist's eyes are the viaduct by which he extends his spirit. His eyes must illustrate his true spirit.

**2)** Spirit — His spirit and attitude are examples of calmness and quiet. He won't rush through a form as if sheer speed results in strength and power. Instead, he will perform his hyung with *thought and purpose.*

**3)** Body — His body should be low, smooth, soft and supple. Low because it gives the martial student strength in his legs for a strong foundation. It stretches his muscles while he's practicing his hyung. And perhaps most important, if he can move quickly and smoothly in a low stance, he will have no trouble attaining speed and agility in a self-defense situation using a higher stance.

It should be noted a soft body doesn't have to be limp. Jwa sae principles dictate the body not be tensed at any time. Kuk sool won practitioners don't believe tenseness is necessary for power. Actually, tenseness stops the flow of ki through the body and greatly limits the body's potential for strength and power. A soft strike performed with speed and focus is all that's necessary for a powerful, penetrating blow.

**4) Feet** — Footwork should be slow and precise, not just in slow motion, but rhythmic and balanced. Emphasis is placed on building a strong foundation which begins with footwork.

**5) Hands** — This final jwa sae determines the hands be swift, agile, sharply defined and precise, especially since the sword is an extension of the hand. It should never be tense force against force. Again, tenseness stops the flow of ki.

If a martial artist is in a ready position with his body soft, his eyes alive, and his internal pressure points (reflecting the flow of his ki) strong, this constitutes jwa sae, and demonstrates how all jwa sae principles interact to produce the final postition.

By first learning jwa sae, the Korean sword practitioner gained control of his body and weapon. Control is dependent upon physical reflexes and mental attitude. The jwa sae taught in present-day kuk sool won are the same techniques Korean warriors learned before they were allowed to make crucial decisions regarding the life or death of their enemies.

The next step in learning Korean sword arts is

called *jung shin*, which means *concentration of mind and spirit*. However, it is far more than mere concentration.

Jung shin begins as an accumulation of proper training under a good teacher of basic etiquette and manners, such as bowing to the national flag and the school, and greeting instructors as "sir." Calling someone "sir" is not meant to teach humbleness. Rather, it serves to remove basic fears people have about showing respect to a senior classmate. When a basic fear is removed, many other fears are also eliminated and the student gains self-confidence. Under jung shin principles, an instructor becomes a guide rather than a superior.

Jung shin is a well-known principle throughout Korean martial arts. It leads the student to achieve a sense of loyalty, self-discipline, self-motivation, self-confidence and purpose. By putting together the esoteric teachings of jung shin, a martial artist can channel his concentration and widsom into a *never-give-up* attitude, an essential in traditional swordsmanship. Jung shin is so important that inferior techniques can still win if he bears superior jung shin.

When the kuk sool student has been prepared both physically and mentally, he proceeds to the third stage — the sword techniques. Korean sword techniques are called *gum sool*. Along with the actual techniques, traditionally the student learns special sword meditation designed to help his mind and body become one with his sword. Meditation is practiced before, during or after sword training. While sitting cross-legged in a lotus position, the sword practitioner continuously strikes downward with his blade thousands of times each day. The effectiveness of any weapon is lessened if the practitioner's mind and body are separate entities.

Sword meditation also serves the practical purpose of giving a student feeling for the sword, how to grip and move it smoothly. Sword meditation serves still another purpose: It develops the martial artist's ki. Most Asian cultures believe ki is the basis of all strength and energy put forth by man. By constantly repeating sword meditations the student eventually learns to transfer his ki into his weapon, giving him seven or more times the strength of a normal person.

Unlike its other Asian brothers, the Korean sword is wielded *both* single-and two-handed. When used with both hands, the intent is to obtain maximum striking power. Two-handed techniques include straight slices which can be vertical, angular, horizontal or upward. Power is generated from the swordsman's muscle and energy, plus a thorough knowledge and application of *joint angle*. He uses his joints, which can actually tie his body together as a unit, at the angle that most effectively works the connecting muscles.

Other two-handed sword techniques are spinning and cutting action requiring the swordsman to turn the weapon with both hands at great speed. In the Korea of ancient times, these techniques were useful

**Sword Turn and Chop**
The defender (on right) stops the attack (1) with a horizontal sword block. He then swings the sword in a circular motion to his right (2) and prepares to fell his attacker (3-5) with a chop to the right side of the neck (6).

Contiuned

17

for both cutting the necks of many enemies at one time and protecting the swordsman's own head by his overhead spinning technique. The power to make work this two-handed technique comes from the speed derived through his body's whiplike momentum.

Low slices to the opponent's ankle are popular jun gum techniques. In the days of actual combat with a bladed weapon, it was sometimes easier to cut down the enemy's foundation than to go for the instant kill. Low cuts can be either single- or two-handed depending on the stylist's body position (jwa sae) at that particular instant. If performed single-handed, power for low cuts depends on the sword-wielder transferring power through the connecting muscles and into the sword. To be effective at such a low angle, the body must function as a single unit.

Every country's sword has straight stabbing techniques. Korean jun gum straight stabs can be either single- or two-handed, depending again on the jwa sae or body position and motion. Kuk sool won's jun gum form teaches both options and helps the martial

student employ either technique. A single-handed
straight stab was most useful in the old days, since
the swordsman's free hand could be used to protect
or block. Often in ancient Korea, the sword's case
was used as a strong blocking device while the
swordsman wielded the blade with his other hand.

Inverted (*yuk gum*) sword techniques are in a
special class. Taught after jun gum principles, yuk
gum uses the sword blade in an inverted position
with the sharp cutting edge facing upward. In ancient
times, yuk gum was a valuable method of close-in
fighting. They *always* began as defensive actions nat-
urally progressing into offensive techniques. While jun
gum techniques are straight action, yuk gum movements are circular and make use of the swordsman's
wrist, elbow and shoulder joints to produce cutting
power. Although there are few double-handed yuk
gum techniques because the movements are short

and circular, most require the use of only one hand to wield the sword. Yuk gum techniques are primarily poking (to the rear) and slicing movements. Slices can be made in all directions, and governed also by the action of the swordsman's wrist, elbow and shoulder joints. Yuk gum techniques are large circular movements; however, while they require the accuracy and precision that characterize jun gum techniques, accuracy here is much more difficult to perfect.

Although swords are not practical everyday weapons today, sword forms and techniques do have practical martial arts applications. For instance, sword forms teach the precision and clarity the martial student can subconsciously apply to his training. When a sword slices through the air it makes a sound. If the sound is heavy or fluttering, it indicates the blade's angle is incorrect and the actual cut would be without cutting strength, similar to hitting with a stick instead of cutting with a knife. If the sound is thin and sharp, then the angle is just right. That sound becomes a learning device for the student. Then, when he works on other facets of martial arts, the concentration and precision gained from practicing his sword forms carries over into his other practice.

Furthermore, as in the old days of sado mu sool martial arts in Korea, when a kuk sool won student first learns the jun gum form, he practices with a wooden sword. However, as he progresses he must switch to a sharp metal blade. If his technique is sloppy, he will cut himself. Students soon learn the value of concise, correct techniques. In the past, the sword was taught primarily as a fighting weapon.

Now, modern martial students repeat that training, not to injure someone, but instead to reinforce the principles which make a true well-rounded martial artist. This practice prepares the student for any situation, and preserves the ancient sword techniques of Korea's past.

# CHAPTER THREE

# Sado Mu Sool's Staff

No stranger to the martial arts of any land, the staff represents one of man's oldest and earliest weapons. Since sado mu sool was the first recorded martial art in Korea, it is the one most likely to have a long history of staff (*bong* in Korean) usage behind it.

Korean staff techniques can be divided into three categories: *dan bong* (short sticks measuring approximately 33 centimeters in length, *joong bong* (a middle-sized staff, 120-140 centimeters long), and *jang bong* (the more common longer staff, 180-220 centimeters).

A famous story about sado mu sool *bong* fighters describes the importance of patterning staff techniques after the fighting habits of the snake. The snake's initial deceptive circling movement as it approaches its prey was patterned after developing a soft, flexible circling motion, completely controlled

23

by the bong practitioner's wrist actions.

When the snake struck, its attack was straight forward and lightning fast. A simulation of the snake's final attack was then added to the staff's circling techniques to produce a sudden, penetrating straight forward attack designed to finish with sharp power.

True Korean staff techniques are often characterized by movements closely resembling those of a snake. An offensive technique is usually a forward movement, while its defensive counterpart involves drawing back the weapon, as if into a coiled position.

While the original sado mu sool bong techniques consisted mainly of basic practical movements common to any terrain and location, staff techniques changed to fit the needs of each kingdom's martial artists.

The Koguryo Kingdom, located in the northern mountains of ancient Korea, developed bong techniques based on its rugged terrain. The jagged mountains of Koguryo cradled narrow winding rivers. To the minds of Koguryo's sado mu sool leaders, the mountains represented offense or attack. Defense was to be found near the protected rivers, which offered speedy escape routes.

Bong techniques followed Koguryo's policy of quick, aggressive retaliation to the enemy's weakest points, using the mountains as its ally. Koguryo staff techniques were powerful, aggressive movements that required a hard strong stick.

While Koguryo bong techniques reflected the power and dominance of mountain strength, they also illustrated, in their defensive movements, the quick slippery escape routines of winding rivers. Staff-wielding bong experts from Koguryo became famous for their strong unrelenting attacks, preceded by deceptive defensive techniques.

The second of the Three Kingdoms, Silla, pursued a different course in the development of its staff techniques.

Since Silla traded extensively with China throughout its reign, its bong techniques reflected much of the exchange between those two friendly kingdoms. In keeping with the influence of Chinese martial arts, the techniques were softer and more circular than those of Koguryo.

Toward the beginning of the Three Kingdom period and shortly before the conquest by Silla over Koguryo and Paekje, Silla entered into a treaty with a small kingdom to the south named Kaya. Kaya's king, Kim Su Lo, was reputed to have been one of the best staff fighters of his time. So good were his techniques the entire kingdom gained a reputation of producing excellent bong-wielders. Through Kaya's treaty and exchange with Silla, Silla Kingdom fighters were greatly influenced by Kim Su Lo's advanced staff usage.

Meanwhile, Paekje developed a different method of staff expertise.

Paekje staff usage involved simple straight forward force-against-force techniques, often lacking the imagination characterizing both Silla and Koguryo bong movements. Paekje fighters used their weapons only as extensions of their arms, with a complete disregard for creative or intricate motion.

Staff techniques merged during the unified Silla period, when Korea became one nation under Silla rule, and remained virtually unchanged until present times.

Bongs in ancient Korea were constructed from a special wood called *pak dahl*, found only in the Sea Jae area of Kyung Bok province. Each staff was treated with an oil that strengthened and preserved the wood. It was steamed to allow the oil to penetrate the wood, forming a strength so mighty it was said even a sharp sword could not cut the pak dahl bong.

The Korean long staff was primarily used as a single-ended weapon, holding it closer to one end, with the other end utilized as the striking surface. Unlike the Chinese double-ended version, which contains many sharp upward and downward techniques, the few double-ended movements seen in jang bong forms are horizontal, with the back and waist used as pivot points.

The joong bong, or middle staff, is the most commonly seen Korean staff. Joong bongs are usually matched to the height of their user. The staff

should measure from between the staff practitioner's eyebrows and the top of his head. Although joong bong techniques are similar to jang bong movements, they aren't restricted by the length of the weapon as are those of the longer jang bong. Therefore, more double-ended and circular spinning techniques are seen in joong bong staff forms.

There are four basic techniques in both jang bong and joong bong training:

**1)** *Ji-ki* — An upward scoop made with the end of the bong. It is designed to be a powerful strike, with the practitioner's body providing momentum.

**2)** *Ji-ru-ki* — A straight poke aimed directly at pressure-point targets. All kuk sool won bong strikes are aimed at vital pressure points. Of the body's 657 pressure points, 47 can be used in the execution of bong techniques.

**3)** *Dol-li-ki* — Softer circling techniques that suddenly thrust into the target.

**4)** *Gul-li-ki* — Basic ground-retrieving techniques played an important role in staff play, since sado mu sool warriors might accidently drop their weapons. These include acrobatic actions, such as shoulder

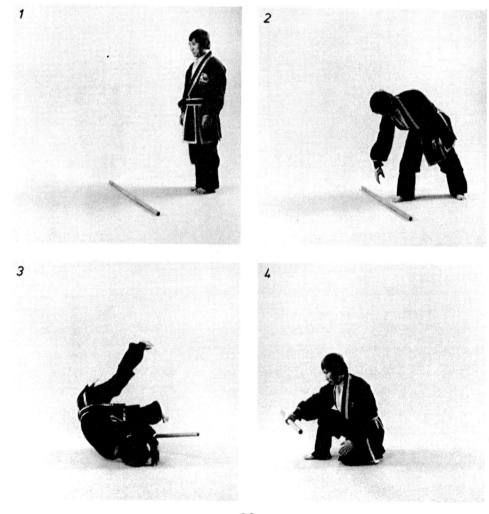

rolls and cartwheels, which enable the bong practitioner to retrieve his weapon and quickly evade an opponent.

Before actual hyungs or staff sparring takes place, *spinning techniques* must be learned. First the staff practitioner stands stationary and moves his bong in spinning patterns. These patterns have the practical training purpose of strengthening and making more flexible the stylist's wrists. There are 15 basic spinning techniques in this stationary position.

Contiuned

Next, both the stylist *and* his bong move with the spinning pattern remaining the same. Now he can practice moving footwork while keeping his weapon in action.

Staff spinning techniques are actually practical offensive and defensive movements. When both ends are used in a double-ended spinning technique, both ends are used for five or six offensive strikes made in quick succession. Each turning and twisting movement provides continuous upward, downward and horizontal strikes to the target.

The dan bong, or short stick, is also classified as a

staff. Although dan bong techniques differ greatly from those of the longer sticks, their pressure-point targets are the same.

Dan bong strikes are different from other bong techniques in two ways. First, although only one stick can be used effectively, they almost always involve the use of *two* short sticks. The initial strike by one stick is not the blow that counts. It is used only to distract the opponent from the *real* attack. The second dan bong then makes almost simultaneous contact with a powerful finishing blow. The second difference between dan bong and other staff techniques is that the short sticks are controlled exclusively by wrist and finger actions. The dan bong is held loosely against the palm, gripped only with the two middle fingers of the hand. The thumb, fore-finger, and little finger actually control the actions of the stick by coordinating with a loose flexible wrist. The dan bong practitioner can quickly change the direction of his attack while striking in rapid-fire succession with either end.

Dan bong strikes are directed at 36 pressure points, with 18 considered lethal. These 18 are called *sa hyul*, and although they are taught in kuk sool won in the first dan bong form, the emphasis is not on killing. Instead, the student is taught the importance of *control*, to use his sa hyul strikes wisely and with danger to his opponent.

Korean staff techniques also reflect a high level of internal *(ki)* training. Using several ki development methods such as meditation, breath control and concentration, the bong stylist learns to direct his own internal energy into his weapon, adding force and penetrating power to his blows.

# CHAPTER FOUR

# The Weapons of Bulkyo Mu Sool

In A.D. 347, China provided the Koguryo Kingdom with an event that strongly influenced Korean history and culture—the introduction of Buddhism, which upholds the cultivation of righteousness in the individual. Following its spread to the Koguryo Kingdom, Buddhism spread rapidly into both Paekje and Silla. As with China, the non-violent Buddhist way of life spawned its forms of martial arts, based originally on exercises designed to promote better health for the sedentary monks. Unlike China, where Buddhist martial arts developed into *revolutionary* kung-fu systems, and were made popular by patriot martial artists fighting against China's oppressive leaders, Buddhist monks in Korea gained the name "defenders of the nation." Korea is the only culture where Buddhist monks were allowed to use a variety of weapons, including bladed weapons, for the actual defense of their kingdoms.

As early as A.D. 660, the Paekje leader, Pok Sin, and a Buddhist monk named Tochim, led over 30,000 warriors in an uprising against oppressive Chinese government officials.

Buddhist monks played an important role in the education of the Silla Kingdom's elite *wha rang* warriors. A Buddhist monk authored the famous *Sesak O Kye* (wha rang five-point code of honor) by which all members structured their lives and fighting careers.

Monks were also skilled in the art of archery. It was a Korean Buddhist monk named Kim Yun Hu who killed the infamous Mongol leader, Sartaq, with an arrow. However, true to his basic non-violent Buddhist nature, when questioned about his accurately placed arrow, Kim Yun Hu remarked it was a "chance" shot, rather than an intended arrow.

While Buddhism influenced Korea during the Three Kingdom era, the Silla Kingdom benefitted most. Buddhist monks with a need for some kind of defense in those troubled times had perfected staff defense and submission techniques.

Buddhist staffs came in all sizes. These tools became valuable weapons to the unarmed and seemingly helpless monks who regularly traveled the roads between villages and monasteries.

The famous Wun Kwang Dae Sa, who was well-versed in martial arts, played an important role in influencing Buddhism in general and staff techniques in particular in the Silla Kingdom. It was Wun Kwang Dae Sa who wrote the five-point code of conduct for the wha rang nobility.

Wun Kwang Dae Sa brought refinement to Silla staff-fighting techniques by incorporating into staff techniques small circular wrist actions, requiring supple wrist movements, along with an emphasis on ki power.

Besides the obvious blocking, striking, and poking techniques, Korean Bulkyo mu sool practitioners added ancient throwing techniques to their staff arsenal. These were accomplished by flipping up an object, such as a stone, into its target with the end of a staff. Seldom did any enemy expect the placid-looking monk to launch a rock with such deadly accuracy. Complete surprise was on the side of the monk.

Bulkyo mu sool also made popular the esoteric staff technique *walking the circle*. Here, monks fighting with a staff always directly faced their opponents and moved in a stalking circle, mirroring every movement made by the opposition. The reasoning behind this strange technique was that the enemy could not defeat a mirror without defeating himself.

This principle of staff fighting, which dictates an enemy can't find any opening in the defender's actions unless he knows his own weaknesses, is carried on in present-day kuk sool won training.

The distance between the walking the circle fighters was always the length of their weapons held at arm's length. The middle of the circle is where the tips of their staffs met.

Most Bulkyo mu sool staff techniques applied to any length weapon. The only exception was the *dan bong* or *short sticks*.

Dan bong techniques differ from other staff techniques because their short length made the targets the body's sensitive pressure points. Also, short sticks are commonly used in pairs, rather than as single weapons.

Short sticks found great popularity with monks who often risked attacks from the thugs and robbers prowling ancient Korea's roads. The sticks became hard penetrating extensions of the martial artist's hands, capable of causing great pain, paralysis,

**Dan Bong (Short Stick) Technique**
From the on-guard position (1), the attacker's staff is blocked (2) when the defender counters with a poke to the solar plexus. He then has two options. He can either attack to the temple (3) or aim for a pressure point on the side of the neck (4).

unconsciousness or even death if the right pressure point was struck.

Dan bong still play an important role in kuk sool won's arsenal of practical self-defense weapons, since they're readily available in today's society in many different forms (rolled magazines, sticks, and implement handles).

Known as *ji pang-ee sool*, cane techniques first became popular in Korean martial arts during the Silla Kingdom. A Buddhist monk, Won Hyo Dae Sa, popularized cane techniques in Korea. One popular story about Won Hyo Dae Sa recounts the time

General Kim Yu Shin (one of the most famous military leaders in Korea's history) lost his son in battle. Won Hyo Dae Sa, using only his cane for defense, entered the chaotic battlefield and retrieved the son's body, bringing it to the General for proper burial.

Cane fighting is a direct descendant of bulkyo mu sool. Many cane techniques were originally developed for use with the bong.

One ancient story tells of how the cane found its way into the world of weapons. A Korean Buddhist monk, walking along the roadside with his cane as a walking aid, found a man with a paralyzed arm lying in the road. The monk poked him in the injured arm at a pressure point with his cane and cured him. The monk reasoned an energy blockage and twisted muscle had paralyzed the man's arm and hitting the central pressure point would dissipate the alien energy. After curing the ailing man, the monk realized not only could he unblock energy channels, but with his stout cane he could strike a pressure point and actually cause paralysis or pain.

The cane became such a popular weapon in ancient Korea that all sorts of versions appeared, including hollowed out examples containing sharp swords or knives. Today, cane techniques vary according to the shape of the stick. Hooked canes and long umbrellas (umbrella-defense techniques are simply modern variations of ancient cane techniques) are useful for stafflike striking and hitting, joint-locking (using leverage from the longer length), grabbing with the hooked end and poking (including pressure-point strikes) with the pointed end.

There are several advantages to a cane or umbrella as a self-defense weapon. First, it's legal to carry. Secondly, no one, including a would-be-attacker, thinks of either a cane or umbrella as a weapon.

A hooked cane has the advantage of length. It can be effective for keeping an attacker at a distance. Both ends are useful, the sharp end for poking or striking and the hooked end for grabbing and choking.

Of course, any direct strike easily can be made, but whether or not a direct strike is effective often depends on what part of the body is the target. Certain areas of the human body are more prone to pain. These are the *pressure points*. Pressure-point strikes are an important part of Korean martial arts. Koreans lead the world in the knowledge and application of pressure-point strikes. So important are pressure-point strikes that kuk sool won starts teaching them at the white belt level.

The cane was useful against almost any attack. It made no difference whether the attack was a grab, kick or punch. Any criminal who attacked a monk carrying a cane took his life in his hands.

The damage inflicted by a cane is determined by the speed with which the technique is administered. This can be very helpful if the defender wants only to stop rather than seriously injure an attacker. If necessary, a cane or umbrella also can become a weapon capable of inflicting serious injury.

Anyone can use a cane as a weapon. It is lightweight, doesn't require much power and comes with a multitude of techniques quickly applied to any situation.

Canes also can be used to administer joint locks by allowing the rigid staff to serve as a brace with which to wrap the assailant's arm and lock his elbow. A hooked-end cane is an excellent grabbing and twisting instrument. The hooked end is the perfect shape for the choke holds and throwing techniques associated with some joint locks.

Several of kuk sool's more common cane self-defense techniques are:

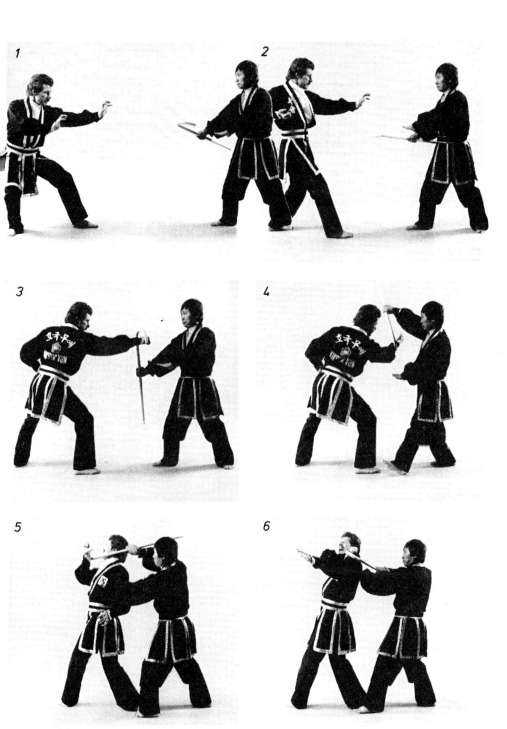

**Cane Technique**
From the square-off position (1), the attacker steps forward with a straight punch (2) that is stopped as the defender hooks (3) his enemy's punching hand. The defender then circles the assailant's trapping hand (4) around his neck (5) and into a submission hold (6) with the attacker's hand wrapped around his neck.

1) — Defense with a hooked-end cane against a punch: Here the cane or long umbrella is used as a hooking and choking weapon. The assailant's punch is stopped by the hooked end of the umbrella or cane, and his punching arm instantly wrapped around his neck in a disabling choke hold. Then, he can be taken down by the leverage of the umbrella and his own arm around his neck.

2) — Defense against a kick and punch combination: The traditional cane defense is to strike the kicking leg at a sensitive pressure point. When the opponent follows with a punch, his punching arm is

**Cane Hook and Trap**
The attacker's kick (1) is blocked by a hard cane strike to a vulnerable section of the ankle. The attacker then attempts (2) a punch, but it is hooked (3) and trapped by the cane.

also struck on a pressure point. Finally, the straight end of the cane is brought down with force upon a pressure point on the top of the assailant's foot, stopping any further attack.

**3)** — A quick-and-easy defense against almost any attack is a quick straight poke to the assailant's stomach followed by a strike down on his head. After the strike to his head, the umbrella or cane is inserted between his legs and pulled to the side in a circular fashion, causing him to spin out of control.

The spear also played a part in the development of Bulkyo mu sool. Since Buddhist monks were

**Cane Takedown Technique**
The attacker prepares (1) to assault the cane practitioner. As he starts his kick, the defender (2) pokes his enemy in the stomach. He then raises his cane (3) and hits (4) him on the head. He finishes (5) by twisting the cane between the attacker's legs and applying (6) a takedown.

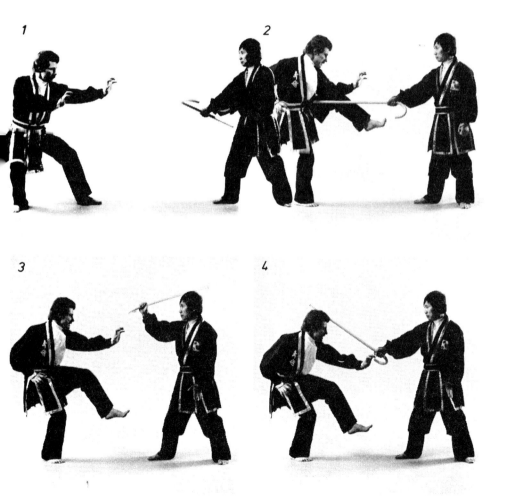

1

2

3

4

Contiuned

regarded as defenders of the nation, whenever an immediate army was needed thousands of monks would take up arms. During times of foreign invasion, the monks were permitted to defend with sharp bladed weapons; the spear was one of the most important.

Already having an extensive knowledge of staff techniques made the fighting monks adept at spear handling. Bulkyo mu sool spear techniques reflected the monk's expertise with the staff. With the exception of a few slicing and poking actions, Bulkyo mu sool spear techniques were basically the same as Bulkyo mu sool staff techniques.

Kuk sool won combines Bulkyo mu sool weapons techniques with those of sado mu sool and koong joong mu sool in each of its weapons forms. From those forms the student receives a flavor of each of Korea's ancient martial arts, while still absorbing the essence of traditional Korean weapons training.

# CHAPTER FIVE

# The Weapons of Koong Joong Mu Sool

Korea's koong joong mu sool (royal court martial art) had many different weapons. However, certain weapons gained more popularity and widespread use. While military officers made use of a variety of weapons, those most preferred were versatile bladed weapons, such as the sword, spear and long-handled moon knife, that could be employed both on the ground or horseback.

The most common military weapon was the sword. Although the sword also had roots in *sado mu sool*, military blades were unique in their own right.

Koong joong mu sool swords came in all shapes and sizes. One Korean general, Lee Soon Shin, was known for his two-meter, nine-centimeter sword, which only the strongest soldiers could wield.

There were seven basic types of koong joong mu sool swords. The most common was called *san-soo-*

43

*do*. It was 129 centimeters in length, with the actual cutting length 99 centimeters, and its handle 30 centimeters long. This sword was one of the most popular with koong joong mu sool fighters and laid the foundation for many of kuk sool won's present-day practice swords. San-soo-do swords had relatively straight single-edged blades. They were designed to be held easily with one or two hands.

Double or twin swords were named *san gum*, referring to the use of two matched blades. San gum's smaller brothers were known as *joong gum* and were midsized double swords, larger than daggers, but not as long as the san gum. Joong gum twin swords were popular within Korea's royal palace and court, since they could be easily concealed.

44

While the average soldier might employ a san-soo-do or its twin equivalent, the san gum, some soldiers in ancient Korea, who relied heavily on their swords for self-defense, preferred the *ah-do*, a sword with a groove running down the length of the blade. This groove added extra strength to the blade by relieving stress as the sword struck down many objects. The ah-do was a heavy sword (over 2,400 grams) with a blade 100 centimeters in length. The blade was sharpened on both sides a few inches at the tip and then along the cutting side to the handle. Its handle measured 33 centimeters.

Another popular military blade was the *hyup-do*, a heavy (1,800 grams), long (131 centimeters) sword with a curved blade. It was a single-edged sword, fit for only the strongest men.

One of the most famous koong joong swords was *bon kuk gum*. Although it originated in the Ko Chosun period, it earned its fame during the time of the Silla Kingdom. An average-sized, single-edged, and slightly curved sword, bon kuk gum weighed between 600 and 1,000 grams. It strongly resembles the swords used for training by today's kuk sool won martial artists.

The last military sword of note was the *yoh-do*, a weapon with a slightly curved blade (100 centimeters in length) and a long handle (90 centimeters). With such a long handle, the bearer certainly had the leverage to cut through just about anything.

Another illustrious koong joong mu sool military weapon was a thick bladed weapon with a stafflike handle, known as *chun jung whule-do* (heavenly dragon moon knife). Although used only by generals, the moon knife became famous throughout the ages through the legends of its users.

The chun jung whule-do was originally designed for use from horseback, and although the moon knife

first became popular in the Koguryo Kingdom, it was known to exist in the Ko Chosun period of 233-108 B.C.

An ancient Korean story tells of a general of Korea's Ko Chosun period who saw a shooting star one dark night during a period when the moon was in a half-moon configuration. He saw the shooting star as a sign of good luck in the making of a special weapon. The shape of the moon became an omen that dictated the shape of that special weapon's blade. Hence the moon knife.

Its name, *heavenly dragon moon knife*, also denotes exclusive use by royalty (Korean generals were always of royal lineage), since dragons are the symbol of Korea's royal court. Many moon knife owners were members of the *sun-bi* warrior class.

The moon knife was developed as the ideal mounted warrior's weapon. It was a long weapon, well over six feet, with a large sharp half-moon-shaped blade at one end. The moon knife's length kept enemy soldiers at a safe distance from the mounted general and his horse. Excellent balance was obtained from a heavy staff end that offset an equally heavy blade. With such a well-balanced

weapon, a mounted soldier could ride at full tilt
through the enemy's ranks, wielding his moon knife
from side to side in a figure-eight pattern. Since the
moon knife was so well-balanced, it also was easy for
the general to remain seated on his mount while
using the weapon.

At one point in Korean history, the moon knife
left the ranks of exclusive use by generals and
became a practical weapon of the average soldier.
Some latter-day Korean armies utilized the long-
handled weapon to bring down enemy cavalry by
cutting its horses' legs. As a foot soldier's weapon, it
was excellent for wading through cavalry. Once its
cutting action began, the moon knife's weight and
momentum kept it going and the bearer moved
smoothly through both people and horses.

Kuk sool won preserves the original whule-do
techniques within its hyungs (forms). One of those
techniques relates directly to koong joong mu sool

history and usage. Called *won* (circle), these techniques are flowery-looking actions. They are circles over the head, figure-eight patterns in front and on either side of the martial artist, and intricate circle patterns.

Despite the popular theory that these techniques are merely fancy performing movements, won techniques did have a practical purpose in ancient Korea. As moon knife-wielding generals rode at full tilt through crowds of enemy soldiers, they needed special techniques to keep their paths clear, hence the figure-eight pattern performed from side to side across the horse's neck.

If the general dismounted, he could keep enemy soldiers at bay with figure-eight patterns directly in front of him and circles made from his front to rear and back again. If any opponent got in the way of the general's twirling moon knife, he immediately lost parts of his anatomy.

Other notable weapons of koong joong mu sool's warrior class were the spear and trident.

# The Spear

Known as *chang* in Korean, the koong joong mu sool spear was both a horse and foot soldier's weapon. It was most popular in three lengths: 220 centimeters, 180 centimeters and 120 centimeters.

The long (220 centimeters) weapon was further broken down into two types: *jang chang*, made with a hardwood staff end, and *jook jang chang*, comprised of a bamboo staff. The hardwood spear was strictly a horseman's weapon, with its end serving as a strong connection between the fast-moving horse and the intended target.

Jook jang chang found its place with foot soldiers who needed a supple spear that would easily bend without breaking, should the target present too much resistance to the foot soldier.

The middle length (180 centimeters) spear was
the sort of in-between size that found no specialized
use. However, the short 120-centimeter weapon
served two specialized purposes. If the soldier was
mounted, he probably carried his army's colors in the
form of a flag attached to the spear head, hence the
name *ki chang* (flag spear). Then, when he needed a
weapon, his short spear with its sharp metal tip was
available. Foot soldiers liked this sized spear since it
was short enough to maneuver easily in crowded
fighting conditions. If the foot soldier needed to carry
two weapons, he could always handle two short
spears.

Koong joong mu sool spear staffs were made from one of three woods: *dae na moo* (bamboo), *bong na moo* and *shin na moo* (light, strong hardwoods).

# Trident

The trident has two names in Korean weaponry. Royal court martial artists referred to it as *dang pah*, and sado mu sool fighters knew it as *san che chang* (three-point spear). Whatever the name, the trident was a heavy weapon, carried only by the strongest warriors.

In koong joong mu sool it was both a foot- and horse-soldier's weapon. Mounted soldiers liked the three-pronged tip, which guaranteed some portion of the target would feel the trident's blade. It was also useful for trapping an enemy's weapon and then pulling it out of his hands, leaving him open for a thrusting attack from the trident's points.

Korean tridents always have a middle tip that is longer than either side tip. This ensures the middle point will spear the enemy, while the side points pin him down.

The two outer prongs of the trident also made it an excellent throwing weapon. Often, if a rival warlord's castle was besieged and the attacker wanted to quickly finish the battle, he might set the castle afire by launching tridents with flaming tips at the walls. Since there were three heavy tips at one end, the trident stayed on a straight course toward its target and was assured to firmly stick in almost any material.

Not only did the koong joong mu sool trident have three sharp tips, but each prong was razor sharp on both sides, making it a double-edged, triple-bladed weapon.

**Trident Trap and Poke**
Armed with a staff, the attacker assaults (1) his enemy by coming overhead with a smash. But as the weapon comes down (2), the defender, armed with a trident, snares (2) the weapon between the fingers of his trident. By jamming the trident toward his attacker (3-5), the defender has total control over the enemy's weapon. The attacker is too busy trying to hold onto the weapon to think about hurting his enemy. When the defender is ready, he just shoves (6) the trident into his enemy's side.

Military weapons comprised only a portion of koong joong mu sool's arsenal. The rest were subtle, easily concealed implements of everyday life which could quickly be brought into defensive use without disturbing Korean royal court culture and habits.

# CHAPTER SIX

# Royal Court Weapons

While weapons for military use took up one section of koong joong mu sool's weaponry, equally as important were the specialized weapons employed by palace guards and royal nobility.

A common practice in ancient Korea was to prohibit the use of military weapons (sword, spear, etc.) within palace confines. This greatly limited the chance of accidental killings of innocent people by overzealous swordsmen. However, some sort of defense was necessary, since hired assassins were constantly employed to dispose of the current ruler.

To keep the tone of royal courts non-military and peaceful in appearance, implements of everyday life became popular koong joong mu sool weapons. For instance, palace guards mastered the art of *po bok sul*, submission techniques utilizing a rope, scarf or belt, to disable an attacker by binding, with a 360-degree wrap, the attacker's arms, legs or throat.

The noblemen of Korea's royal courts found the common fan an excellent weapon for immediate self-defense situations. Easily carried and useful in everyday life, the fan filled nobility's need for an *instant and ever-present* weapon.

With techniques borrowed from Bulkyo mu sool, the innocent cane also became a popular koong joong mu sool weapon.

Even royal court ladies had access to effective weapons of self-defense. Aside from the fan, twin short swords *(dan sang gum)* found great favor with both men and women of Korea's aristocratic classes.

## The Rope

As early as A.D. 1400, palace guards employed rope submission techniques *(po bok sul)* to capture and subdue any trespassers. Forbidden to carry bladed weapons, guards instead wore lengths of harmless looking rope. The art of po bok sul became so popular among professional peacekeepers it has been handed down through the ages and is extensively used today in law enforcement agencies throughout Korea. The rope is considered an important traditional weapon and is taught in all kuk sool won schools. There is a po bok sul technique for use against any offensive strike or grab.

Rope-tying techniques are quick circular wrapping movements designed to effectively bind any portion of the opponent's body. The rope is also used to block punches and kicks the instant before it is used to encircle and trap an opponent.

In the old days, rope techniques found favor because they were swift, silent, and completely disabling techniques, designed to quickly kill an assailant and then move on to the next attacker without any sound of attack. Today, practitioners strive to employ po bok sul only as a means of submission,

Contiuned

**Rope Block and Wrap**
From the on-guard position (1), the rope stops (2) the attacker's kicks as it acts as a crossblock. The ensuing punch (3) is blocked as the defender wraps (4-5) the rope around his attacker's wrist. The attacker is then placed (6) into a submission hold by circling (7-8) his wrapped arm around his neck.

without actually injuring the attacker. This makes rope tying extremely popular with law enforcement agencies. For instance, although most po bok sul techniques end with the assailant's neck wrapped securely with the rope, his arm or hand is *always* positioned between the rope and his neck to prevent choking.

Rope-tying techniques allow the defender to tie his attacker and leave him while he goes for help, secure in the knowledge the assailant will still be there when he returns.

All koong joong mu sool rope-tying techniques are designed as *safe control* techniques. They employ the advanced techniques of pressure point and joint locking in conjunction with the rope, scarf or belt. Po bok sul techniques are unique because, with the exception of firearms, modern man has not improved on these ancient Korean subduing techniques.

## The Fan

In Korea, the fan was one of the favorite weapons of nobility in royal courts where conventional weapons were banned. As a weapon, the fan gained its greatest popularity during the Three Kingdom

period. At that time, the fan became a convenient, elegant and deceptive weapon of Korea's royal martial artists.

The fan is a *convenient* weapon, since it is small and lightweight. When held, the fan was easily available and ready for almost any situation. When not at his fingertips, it could be easily and quickly concealed in his loose, flowing outer garments.

A fan could be utilized in many different ways by its Korean handler. It was effective either open or closed, with the butt end, sides and tip equally useful as striking surfaces.

Since the fan was a nobleman's weapon, it had to

**Fan Block and Counter**
The attacker prepares (1) his assault. His kick is then blocked (2) with a pressure-point strike to the side of the ankle. Next, his punch is blocked (3) by one fan while the other is brought up (4) for a jab to the throat (5) and a pressure-point strike (6) to the side of the neck.

**1**

**2**

**3**

**4**

**5**

**Fan Block and Counter**
From the ready position (1), the
attacker's kick is blocked (2) by
hitting a pressure point on top
of his kicking foot with the butt
end of the fan. The fan then
deflects (3) the punch by striking a pressure point on the wrist
(4). The defender finishes the
fight (5) by poking the attacker
in the solar plexus with the
fan's butt end.

be elegantly constructed. It was often made of the finest silk with silver or gold inlay to highlight the bright colors and patterns imprinted on its body. Feathers from exotic birds added a graceful finishing touch to the fan's design.

The Korean fan was a deceptive weapon because it didn't look like a powerful fighting tool. However, the power generated with it can cut deeply and break bones.

Fans were often geared to give their users more killing power. Sometimes metal strips were placed on the fan's outer edges and in each fold, giving the innocent-looking fan extra striking and cutting power.

Small finger-sized knives were occasionally inserted into the feathers at the fan's tip. When the feathers brushed across an enemy's face, he felt the sting of many sharp knives. These same knives could also be strategically employed within the folds of the folded fan. When suddenly whipped open, the knives shot out into the enemy's vital points.

Poison sacks that broke when the fan was opened were another popular addition to the feathers. This poison caused symptoms ranging from irritation and blindness to death. Korea's fan weapons were usually constructed of a special hardwood known as *pak dahl*. Today, Korean fans are made of bamboo. While not as strong as pak dahl, bamboo fans are still sturdy enough to break several stacked boards.

The primary theory of fan techniques is transferring the martial artist's *ki* (internal energy) out through his hands and into the fan. With speed and precision, the fan becomes a formidable weapon.

The angle of attack between the fan and its opponent must also be correct and targeted toward a pressure point to make the strike disabling. Therefore, a good fan stylist is knowledgeable in the loca-

**Fan-Fighting Techniques**
In this example of fan-fighting techniques, one fan provides (1) extra leverage for a shoulder lock, while the other places (2) pressure on a pressure point high on the attacker's arm. With the attacker in a shoulder lock, the butt end of one fan is raised high (3) and brought down on a pressure point at the base of the neck.

tion and response of pressure points and in the mechanical aspects of the angles of attack.

Striking surfaces of the fan are the sides, tail or butt end, and the tips of its ribs when opened. The sides of a folded fan are used to block an oncoming kick or punch.

# Twin Short Swords

In some instances, very short bladed weapons were allowed within palace walls. These were usually easily concealed twin short swords, known as *dan sang gum*. Dan sang gum were the shortest version of

any double swords.

The ladies of Korea's royal courts often required bodyguards who could easily gain admittance to their sleeping quarters and dressing areas. For those reasons, the bodyguards were also women. They often carried lightweight twin short swords within their flowing outer garments. The length of most dan sang gum was approximately 30 centimeters, with the width of each blade about ten centimeters. While the length and width were fairly standard, the actual shape varied. Some had single-edged blades and others resembled daggerlike, double-edged weapons.

They all bore protective hand guards, approximately ten centimeters in diameter. The actual intended use of the dan sang gum determined the size and shape of the weapon. If the female guard needed to bury her weapons beneath the many folds of her royal garment, she might prefer short swords with small handguards which wouldn't become entangled in the material of her dress. Guards, both male and female who might be actively involved in battle situations against military weapons, such as long swords and spears, chose swords with larger, more protective handguards. Female bodyguards of very high position within the royal courts even had their own handmaidens whose only task was to carry the guard's short swords.

There are three ways to properly hold twin short swords. The first is called *jun*, and is a straight forward position where the blade is pointed forward, as with a knife, and the handguards are positioned below and around the fingers for protection.

The second method is *yuk* (inverted). Here the blades are reversed, with the points aimed toward the rear. The handguard now lies on top of the hand. The yuk position was a popular defensive technique, using the strength of the blade to block blows from

other weapons. Yuk was also useful for close-in fighting, where there wasn't enough room to use the full length of the defender's arms with her swords in the jun position.

The final holding technique was a combination *jun* and *yuk*, where one sword was positioned defensively in the yuk position, and the other offensively in the straight or jun position. This was called *jun-yuk* (one straight and one inverted).

## Cane

Although the cane had its origins in Bulkyo mu sool, royal court martial arts found it to be a most

useful weapon, especially when the fighter wanted to carry an outwardly innocent-looking weapon.

Basic koong joong mu sool cane techniques were the same as with Buddhist martial arts. However, Buddhist monks, unless they were involved in defending their country, were mainly interested in submission techniques.

Such was not the case in the royal palace. A fighting encounter in any of Korea's royal palaces was sure to be a life-or-death situation. For that reason, canes were improved with swords hidden in the

**Cane Technique**
The attacker approaches (1) the defender who is armed with a cane. They square off (2). As the assailant kicks, the defender hooks the kicking leg with his cane, pulling him off balance. Next the attacker's knife slash (3) is blocked as the defender hooks and immobilizes the knife arm. The defender reaches forward (4) to hook the cane around the attacker's neck (5). This final movement (6-7) places him in a chokehold.

1

2

3

4

Continued

long end of the cane, or a poisoned blade protruding from the cane's tip.

Koong joong mu sool cane techniques also differed from their Buddhist counterparts in that royal court martial artists used *only* offensive techniques involving many cutting and slashing actions.

The cane techniques taught today in kuk sool won are a combination of both Bulkyo mu sool and koong joong mu sool, utilizing many Buddhist defense and submission actions alongside royal court offensive techniques. However, the practice of improving canes with hidden knives is forbidden in kuk sool won.

# CHAPTER SEVEN

# Jung Gum Hyung

(Straight Sword Form)

**1**—Attention position (feet together). Bow to front, left hand grips sword scabbard.

**2**—Left foot steps back into right kneeling position. Right hand grips sword handle, preparing to draw the sword.

**3**—Begin drawing sword from scabbard.

**4**—Sword drawn from scabbard, cutting edge of blade angled 45 degrees upward.

**5**—Completion of drawing cut. Place scabbard on the ground.

**6**—Bring sword down centerline, both hands gripping. Note: The tip of the blade is at eye level.

**7**—Sword in same position. Stand upright into a right front stance.

**8**—Bring the left foot forward into an attention position.

**9**—Draw sword back over head to prepare for a downward cut.

**10**—Completion of drawing back
action.

**11**—Cut down centerline.

**12**—Step forward into a right front stance. Pull sword back over head, lining up the blade with the center of the spine.

**13**—Completion of downward cut to front centerline.

**14**—Right foot steps back into an attention stance. Begin drawing the sword back.

**15**—Complete drawing the sword back and over head.

**16**—Cut down and at a 45-degree
angle to the right side of the body.

**17**—Left hand blocks to the front,
horizontally to the ground.

**18**—Rotate the sword back and over
the head, bracing the back of the
blade against the left hand.

**19**—Bring the sword vertical to the
ground on the right side of the body.
Left hand still braces the blade.

**20**—Stab behind on the right.

**21**—Bring sword to front, blocking upward.

**22**—Begin a horizontal cut to the left.

**23**—Horizontal cut to left halfway
completed.

**24**—Completion of horizontal cut to the left.

**25**—Turn blade so the cutting edge is facing outward, away from the body.

**26**—Cut horizontally, in front of the body, to the right.

**27**—Circle sword counterclockwise horizontally above the head.

**28**—Cut horizontally to the left. Left
hand braces right hand for added
strength.

**29**—Circle sword clockwise horizontally above head.

**30**—Cut horizontally to right side.
Left hand braces right hand.

**31**—Circle sword overhead counterclockwise. Left foot steps to the left.

**32**—Cut horizontally to the left at neck level. Left front stance.

**33**—Pivot 180 degrees clockwise into left kneeling position. Prepare for a horizontal cut.

**34**—Horizontal cut at knee level.

**35**—Stand up and step forward with left foot into a square horse stance. Rotate sword downward to right. Left hand to left, palm facing outward.

**36**—Draw sword back and over the
head. Brace blade with the left hand.

**37**—Stab six inches downward at a
45-degree angle.

**38**—Pivot 180 degrees clockwise into
a right front stance. Grab sword grip
with both hands and prepare for a cut
downward.

**39**—Downward cut to centerline.

**40**—Left foot steps forward into square horse stance. Same as #35.

**41**—Left hand braces sword over head. Same as #36. Stab six inches downward at a 45-degree angle.

**42**—Pivot 180 degrees into a right
front stance. Draw sword back over
head. Prepare for downward cut.

**43**—Cut downward to centerline.
Right front stance.

**44**—Pivot counterclockwise into square horse stance. Move 360 degrees counterclockwise with sword blade, using wrist rotation. Left hand protects next to the blade.

**45**—Pick up right leg into modified crane stance (knee angled inward).

**46**—Rotate sword 360 degrees counterclockwise, using wrist rotation.

**47**—Right foot steps down into square horse stance. Left palm behind back of blade.

**48**—Pick up right leg into round kick
position. Rotate sword blade 360
degrees counterclockwise.

**49**—Brace back of sword tip with top
of foot.

**50**—Kick sword straight out, cutting up centerline.

**51**—Right leg steps down into a square horse stance. Circle sword counterclockwise over head.

**52**—Horizontal cut across body to
left at midsection level.

**53**—Completion of horizontal cut.
Turn cutting edge of blade away from
body.

**54**—Horizontal cut to right side of body. Square horse stance.

**55**—Horizontal cut to left at neck level.

**56**—Turn blade to opposite direction
and cut 45 degrees downward, across
body to right.

**57**—Horizontal cut downward to left
at knee level.

**58**—Rotate sword counterclockwise
to right. Left hand blocks, palm facing
out, to left of body.

**59**—Right foot steps back into left
cross-stance.

**60**—Draw sword over head. Left
hand braces tip.

**61**—Grip sword with both hands.

**62**—Begin 45-degree downward cut to left side.

**63**—Completion of 45-degree downward cut.

**64**—Begin to pivot clockwise. Circle sword clockwise over head.

**65**—Complete pivot into square horse stance. Sword prepares for 45-degree downward cut.

**66**—Begin 45-degree downward cut to right.

**67**—Completion of downward cut.

**68**—Left hand forward, palm facing out. Right front stance.

**69**—Left foot steps forward into modified back stance (weight 50-50). Begin to circle sword downward to rear.

**70**—Complete circle by drawing
sword back and over head.

**71**—Tip of blade positioned over left
fingertips.

72—Right hand to waist. Prepare to
stab. Left hand lines up sword blade.
Note: Left hand does not touch blade.

73—Step forward with right foot into
long right front stance. Stab straight
to midsection. Left hand braces right
hand.

**74**—Pivot to left into square horse
stance. Rotate sword blade 360
degrees counterclockwise, using wrist
rotation. Left hand behind blade.

**75**—Pick up right leg into modified
crane stance.

**76**—Rotate sword counterclockwise 360 degrees.

**77**—Jump back into square horse stance. Left palm behind sword, but not touching blade.

**78**—Left foot steps to right 180 degrees. Body is now directly behind the sword blade, facing opposite direction.

**79**—Horizontal cut to right at mid-section level.

**80**—Jump and spin body clockwise
360 degrees. At same time rotate
sword blade clockwise over head.

**81**—Land in square horse stance.

**82**—Horizontal cut to the right.

**83-85**—Rotate sword 360 degrees counterclockwise.

**84**

**85**

**86**—Prepare for horizontal cut by
bringing blade upward.

**87**—Horizontal cut to left across
midline.

**88**—Horizontal cut to right across midline.

**89**—Rotate sword 360 degrees counterclockwise, using wrist action.

**90**—Point tip of blade downward
and to the rear.

**91**—Bring sword back behind the
back, with the blade lined up with the
spine, tip of blade pointing upward.

**92**—Bring sword to front of body.

**93**—Cut upward with cutting edge of
blade facing up.

**94**—Prepare for horizontal cut to the left.

**95**—Horizontal midline cut to the left.

**96**—Horizontal midline cut to the right.

**97**—Left foot comes together with right foot, knees bent slightly. Right hand to right side. Left hand forward, lined up with tip of blade, but not touching the blade.

**98**—Bend knees more, thrust sword
blade forward. Left hand braces right
hand for more power.

**99**—Begin to draw sword back
toward body. Left hand at right side,
palm down.

**100**—Right hand draws sword
upward, tip of blade angled down
slightly. Left hand braces back of
blade. Note: In this movement, the
left hand actually touches the back of
the sword blade.

**101**—Thrust straight to the rear.

**102**—Left foot steps back to drop
into a left kneeling position. Sword is
still thrust behind.

**103**—Draw sword out and forward,
cutting upward. Pick up scabbard.
You should now be back in the same
location as in the beginning of the
hyung.

**104**—Stand up into a right front
stance, sword positioned in front.
Scabbard is held in the left hand.

**105**—Begin to line up sword with
scabbard opening.

**106**—Tip of sword lines up.

**107**—Sheath sword into scabbard.

**108**—Bow.

# CHAPTER EIGHT

# Joong Bong Hyung

(Middle Staff Form)

**1**—Attention position.

**2-3**—Preparing for staff bowing position.

**4**—Bow to front.

**5**—Staff in vertical position, both hands together, right hand on top.

**6**—Left foot steps back into a front stance.

**7**—Staff is brought downward to the left side.

**8**—Continuation of left side movement.

**9**—Beginning of right side downward movement.

**10**—Continuation of right side
movement, near completion of first
figure eight.

**11**—Without stopping action from
the previous figure eight, the staff is
brought downward to the left side.

12—The left side is completed and
the staff is brought over to the right
side to start the figure eight on that
side.

13—Continuation of right side
movement, near completion of figure
eight.

**14**—Completion of right side movement, bring the staff down the center preparing for a strike to the centerline.

**15**—Finishes two figure eights with a downward strike that does not stop, but instead moves into the next movement.

**16**—Beginning of single-hand figure
eight. Left foot steps forward to attention position (feet together). Right
hand grips staff in the middle. Left
hand parallels center of body.

**17-20**—Single-hand figure eight from
left side to right side with the right
hand holding the staff.

**18**

**19**

**20**

**21-24**—Same as 17-20. Single-hand figure eight from left side to right side with the right hand holding the staff.

**22**

**23**

**24**

**25**—Left hand grabs the upper portion of staff (staff is in vertical position).

**26**—Left foot steps back to right front stance. Staff is brought down to waist level, horizontal to ground.

**27**—Left hand pulls staff around the waist (maintain body contact with the staff). Right hand positioned defensively in front.

**28**—Both feet pivot into a left front stance. Staff is against waist on the the left side.

**29**—Continue pivoting into a cross-stance. Note: From 26-29, the twisting body action has moved the staff 360 degrees.

**30**—Right hand grabs the staff in the middle. The staff is still horizontal to the waist.

**31**—Right hand pulls staff around the waist to the right. Start to pivot body clockwise into left front stance.

**32**—Complete the pivot into a left front stance.

**33**—Continue pivoting from a left front stance into a right front stance. Staff is still horizontal against the waist.

**34**—Right hand pulls the staff outward to the right.

**35**—Left hand grips the staff, next to
the body, with the palm facing
upward.

**36**—Staff moves downward to the
left side.

**37**—Staff makes one revolution on
the left and then back to the middle.

**38**—Continues downward to the right.

**39**—Figure eight is near completion.

**40**—Complete figure eight with a downward strike to the centerline.

**41**—Beginning of 360-degree rotation around the head.

**42**—180 degrees of the 360-degree circle completed.

**43**—Nearing completion of 360-degree circle.

**44**—Completes the 360-degree rotation with a focused strike to the temple area.

**45**—Drop into a left kneeling position. Begin 360-degree rotation around head.

**46**—Nearing completion of 360-degree circle around head.

**47**—Completes 360-degree rotation with a focused strike to the knees.

**48**—Change right hand position into palm facing downward. Bring front end of staff down sharply with right hand.

**49**—Continue above motion into a strike to the rear using the front end of the staff.

**50**—Right hand pulls the rear portion
of the staff toward the front and into
an upward strike.

**51**—Right hand pulls the front end of
the staff down and into an upward
strike to the rear.

**52**—Push downward with the right
hand, bringing the staff into an
upward strike to the front. Note: This
is the same movement as #50, but on
the right side of the body.

**53**—Stand up into a right front
stance, staff held in front with both
hands.

**54**—Downward to left side.

**55**—Continuation of #54.

**56**—Completion of left side.

**57**—Downward beginning of right side.

**58**—Continuation of right side, figure
eight near completion.

**59**—Completion of figure eight with
downward strike to centerline.

**60**—Bring left foot forward into
attention stance (feet together). Staff
is in vertical position. Left hand grabs
the top portion of the staff.

**61**—Left foot steps behind and to the
side to prepare to pivot the body 180
degrees counterclockwise.

**62**—Complete pivot 180 degrees
with a horizontal strike to the temple.
Right hand in front on the staff.

**63**—Turn the right hand around on
the staff with the palm facing upward.

**64**—Begin to raise staff, front end up.

**65**—With staff in a horizontal position, the left hand grabs the top of the staff, palm facing away from the body.

66—Bring the left foot forward to an attention stance. The staff is still in a horizontal position.

67—The left foot steps back and to the side, preparing to pivot 180 degrees counterclockwise.

**68**—Pivot 180 degrees counterclockwise with the staff brought up horizontal to the body, striking to the
midsection.

**69**—The left foot steps in front of the
right foot into a left cross-stance. The
staff is held horizontal at chest level.

**70**—Poke to the right to the midsection with the front end of the staff.

**71**—The right foot slides around and in front of the left into a right cross-stance.

**72**—Pivot 180 degrees counterclockwise with the staff striking horizontally to the neck region.

**73**—Left foot steps forward into an
attention position facing the same
direction as the beginning movement
of the hyung. Rotate staff to bring it
into a vertical position, right hand on
top.

**74**—Rotate staff clockwise into a
horizontal position at chest level.

**75**—Bow to the front.

**76**—Bring staff back into vertical
position.

## In Hyuk Suh

When the Japanese occupied Korea in 1910, they forced master instructors of Korea's Royal Court Army, such as Myung Duk Suh, into hiding in fear of their lives. Martial arts practice was strictly forbidden in Japanese-occupied Korea. Myung Duk Suh returned to his home in the Taegu area and secretly taught only his immediate family.

The Suh family had practiced martial arts for 16 generations, and when Myung Duk Suh's young grandson, In Hyuk Suh, showed promise, his grandfather concentrated his attention on him. His serious martial arts education began when he was only five years old.

Suh was still very young when his grandfather was killed during the Korean conflict. However, his grandfather had arranged special continued training from many different teachers, comprising backgrounds in all three Korean foundation martial arts: sado mu sool, Bulkyo mu sool, and koong joong mu sool.

In the late 1950s, In Hyuk Suh combined his training and organized and systemized Korea's scattered martial art techniques into one single system, appropriately named *kuk sool won (Korean national martial art association)*. Kuk sool won grew rapidly in Korea, finding favor not only with native Koreans eager to rediscover ancient traditional martial arts, but with American servicemen who also saw the practical side of this training.

In Hyuk Suh came to the United States in 1974 to establish kuk sool won as the world's leading traditional Korean martial arts system, with emphasis placed on all forms of self-defense along with complete mental and physical conditioning.

## Jane Hallander

Jane Hallander is a photojournalist who has written over 200 martial arts articles for magazines around the world. She is the author of *The Complete Guide to Kung Fu Fighting Styles* and *Choy Li Fut Kung Fu,* and has practiced martial arts for many years.